Word Groupings

GEORGE HILL AND MERIEL BOWERS

HEINEMANN
EDUCATIONAL

Heinemann Educational Publishers
Halley Court, Jordan Hill, Oxford OX2 8EJ
a division of Reed Educational & Professional Publishing Ltd

MELBOURNE   AUCKLAND
FLORENCE   PRAGUE   MADRID   ATHENS
SINGAPORE   TOKYO   SAO PAULO
CHICAGO   PORTSMOUTH (NH)   MEXICO
IBADAN   GABORONE   JOHANNESBURG
KAMPALA   NAIROBI

British Library Cataloguing in Publication Data

Hill, George
  Teeline word groupings.
  1. Shorthand——Teeline
  I. Title II. Bowers, Meriel
  653'.428   Z56.2.T4

  ISBN 0–435–45326–2

Printed in England by Clays Ltd, St Ives plc

Contents

Other Teeline titles available

Teeline: Revised Edition by I. C. Hill and Meriel Bowers
Teeline Shorthand Made Simple by Harry Butler
Teeline Word List by I. C. Hill
First Teeline Workbook: Revised Edition by I. C. Hill and Meriel Bowers
Second Teeline Workbook: Revised Edition by I. C. Hill and Meriel Bowers
Teeline Shorthand Dictation Passages by Dorothy Bowyer
Teeline Dictation and Drill Book by I. C. Hill and G. S. Hill
Handbook for Teeline Teachers edited by Harry Butler
Medical Teeline by Pat Garner and Pat Clare
New Teeline Dictation Book edited by George Hill

Part One
Introduction

Those of us who were fortunate enough to witness the birth of Teeline and to have had the opportunity of helping it through its infancy have an abiding memory of the enthusiasm it generated in our students. Almost without exception they thoroughly enjoyed learning the system and it was by no means unusual for students to ask their teacher at the end of the course if there was some way in which they could help to 'spread the message'.

One such student, having reached an examination standard 80 w.p.m. on a course of 42 hours' tuition in seven weeks, volunteered to give a talk to an audience of shorthand teachers and to answer their questions. They asked her what textbooks she and her teacher had used, when had 'theory' lessons ended and speed-building begun, how many hours she had spent drilling outlines and how much homework she had done.

She truthfully answered that no textbooks had been used because none had yet been published, that speed-building in the form of dictation had begun in the second lesson when the students knew as much as was needed to write simple sentences, that she did not understand what they meant by 'drilling', and that she had done no real homework—'I just practised taking down what people said.'

It is not our intention to argue that Teeline should be taught or learned without the aid of a good textbook: the student mentioned above might have done even better had one been available. Neither do we believe that dictation has to start in the second lesson, that drilling is never a beneficial exercise or that no student ever needs to be given homework.

What we want to stress as strongly as possible is that a student's success depends in no small measure on the teacher's attitude to the subject—an attitude that will be very quickly discerned by the student and, in all probability, adopted without question. Acquiring the right attitude—one that derives from what may be called the 'philosophy' of Teeline—is never a problem for the teacher who has not previously taught a different system, but 'converts' (for want of a better term) can find it very difficult.

There are a number of ways in which their inability to shed old attitudes can manifest itself: a Teeline principle may be called a rule, a student's outline may be described as wrong simply because it is different from the textbook outline, excessive use may be made of generally inappropriate techniques such as drilling, students may be made to spend more time reading textbook outlines than reading their own notes, and so on.

Teeline Word Groupings

We would be exceeding our brief if we attempted to do more than direct attention to the fact that embracing the Teeline philosophy—already expounded in several Teeline books—inevitably leads to better teaching, better learning and better results. Our particular concern is, of course, that this book should be used by both teachers and students to the best possible advantage. We therefore urge all readers to give serious consideration to the following points:

1 A single principle may generate an untold number of groupings.
2 Any grouping is just an example of the application of one or more principles.
3 No student should ever be coerced into using a specific grouping.
4 All students should be encouraged to use groupings and to devise their own outlines.
5 A drill is a useful tool for boring holes and shorthand students!

1. Word-groupings: Their Nature, Functions and Value

A word-grouping consists of two or more words written as one; or, in traditional shorthand terminology, two or more outlines written as one. Joining words together is not a phenomenon peculiar to fast writing systems: the English language is rich in compound words such as *windmill, gunpowder, nevertheless, classroom*, and even *shorthand* itself. In fact, the creation of compound words is a continuous process, recent examples including *motorway, hovercraft, checkout* and *overkill*.

Sometimes a couple of words will enjoy a period of engagement—signified by a hyphen—before being joined in linguistic matrimony. Incidentally, some couples remain permanently engaged (*tailor-made, easy-going*) while others have uncertain wedding dates because of disagreement among lexicographers (some dictionaries give *by-pass*, others *bypass*).

Whether hyphenated or joined, words are linked to show that they are to be treated as one word with one meaning and, indeed, are to be read as such. Thus we can convey in speech the difference between a *black bird* and a *blackbird*, a *cross word* and a *crossword*, a *little used child's toy* and a *little-used child's toy*, an *ill fated woman*, and an *ill-fated woman*, a man who is *cleaning up in the bedroom* and a man who is *cleaning-up in the bedroom*. These important differences in meaning are conveyed by variations in stress and hiatus: we say *black* (pause) **bird** or **black**bird. In writing, a comma may sometimes be used to denote a pause: an *ill, fated woman*, a man who is *cleaning, up in the bedroom*.

Clearly, there are times when the shorthand writer will find it difficult to produce an accurate and unambiguous transcript unless the notes are a record not only of the words uttered but also of their intended meaning. This can be done by punctuating the notes with hyphens and commas, and by using any distinctive mark or symbol to show a stressed word or syllable. Another method, however, is the use—or

deliberate non-use—of word-groupings: An ill, fated woman ...𝑛 𝐶 𝜎 ⌣𝑛..., but an ill-fated woman ...𝑛 𝐺 ⌣𝑛......... . In the former, the deliberate non-use

of the grouping indicates that meaningful pause made by the speaker. Similarly, the ambiguity of *I saw it before the girl answered* can be resolved by not using the grouping

before the ...𝓐𝓵...... if the meaning was *'I saw it before,' the girl answered*.

3

Teeline Word Groupings

Resolving ambiguities is not, of course, the most common function of word-groupings, and the above examples can also be viewed as demonstrating the general rule that transcribing is facilitated when groupings are consonant with the 'natural' patterns formed by the words spoken. Almost any sentence will contain consecutive words that have an affinity for each other—they just seem to go together naturally. Most of the outlines in this book are of natural word-groupings of which three common types are worth mentioning here.

The first consists of a pronoun and verb: *I am, we were, you will, there are, it is*, etc. Very often these form a basis for longer groupings: *I am sorry, you will be, it is not possible, there is no doubt.*

The second type is a verb in the infinitive: *to be, to see, to go, to say.*

The third is the hackneyed phrase, cliché or much-used expression: *to some extent, in this day and age, from time to time, at the end of the day, more or less, come straight to the point, in my opinion.* A particular advantage of this third type is that some of the letters, syllables or words can often be omitted to give a faster but still readable outline:

from time to time ....…, more or less ....…, to some extent ....… .

The fact that natural groupings possess certain merits does not mean that other kinds of groupings are necessarily valueless; in fact, disagreement about whether or not a certain grouping is a natural one is not uncommon. What matters most is the advantage to be gained by its use, and the advantage sought by all Teeline writers is an increase in speed with no loss of readability.

However, as groupings vary enormously in their effectiveness as speed-builders it is helpful to have some way of evaluating them. A simple way for any Teeline writer to find out if a grouping is worthwhile is to compare the number of times it can be written in 30 seconds with the number of times the separate words can be written in

30 seconds. For example, if ....… can be written 24 times and

...............… 8 times then it is a worthwhile grouping because it trebles the

writing speed. Similarly, if ....… can be written 56 times and ....… 28

times there is a doubling of writing speed. It would be quite wrong, however, to assume from this evidence that the grouping for *come straight to the point* is of more value to the writer than the grouping for *of the*.

When comparing the value of two different groupings—each of which may be worthwhile—we must take into account the frequency with which they are likely to occur and, as there is a dearth of information on the subject, a little private research and intelligent guesswork is usually needed.

It is important to select appropriate source material because the frequency of many groupings is at least partly determined by the nature of the material: the insurance office secretary will not glean much useful information from the local journalist's notebook, nor the medical secretary from the correspondence file in a shipping office. Having gathered the material—the more the better—and having decided on the groupings to be researched, it becomes a simple counting exercise aimed at discovering how many times each grouping occurs. If, for example, *come straight to the point* occurs once in 10,000 words and *of the* occurs 60 times (an average of once every 167 words) we can confidently assume that the latter is a more valuable grouping than the former.

As a matter of interest, a 100 w.p.m. writer saves about 2.20 seconds (worth some 3.70 words) every time ...⌒̇........ is written, and a little less than 0.60 seconds (one word) every time ....] .... is written. Therefore, if the frequency of *of the* was only four times that of *come straight to the point* it would still be the more valuable grouping.

The above comparison of a very common and a fairly uncommon grouping was chosen to demonstrate the point that frequency of occurrence is the most important factor to consider when assessing the value of a grouping. Of course, most Teeline teachers and experienced writers would find the counting procedure unnecessary in such a case: it is obvious that *of the* is by far the more common grouping. In most cases, however, the intelligent guess will be found wanting.

Suppose we want to discover the relative values of a number of different groupings. We have already found out by 30-second drilling that they are all more or less equally worthwhile, but their frequency 'pecking order' is not at all obvious. To complicate matters we also wish to know whether these groupings are of more value to the general secretary, the medical secretary, the legal secretary or the journalist. We collect our material—an equal number of words from each source— and count the number of times each grouping occurs. The totals can then be displayed in simple tabular form.

The results obtained from just such a piece of research are set out in the table on page 6, but it should be noted that as the source material consisted of only 4,000 words from each occupational group it would be unwise to regard small frequency differences (perhaps less than 5 occurrences) as significant.

There are several interesting points to consider when interpreting the data in the table. Is the grouping *of the* especially valuable to legal secretaries? If so, why? Or is 42 a freak result caused by the small sample? In general, do journalists stand to gain most by using these groupings? If so, is it because their work is less specialized? Would the figures for journalists have been substantially different if their source material had consisted wholly of court reports?

Teeline Word Groupings

Bearing in mind that the ten groupings are non-specialized, do the results of this research support the contention that the frequency of a grouping will vary with the type of material studied? Why is the medical secretary's score much higher than average for *in the* and *over the*, but well below average for five other groupings? How would other groupings of the same type (*after the, before the, as the, about the, into the*, etc.) have compared with the ten studied?

	General secretary	Medical secretary	Legal secretary	Journalist	Total (16,000 words)
of the	23	24	42	27	116
in the	13	29	16	16	74
on the	9	3	23	11	46
from the	11	2	6	16	35
for the	16	3	6	10	35
to the	6	2	11	16	35
with the	11	6	6	6	29
that the	2	6	4	11	23
at the	3	2	6	11	22
over the	1	9	1	4	15
Total (4,000 words)	95	86	121	128	430

This section has been concerned with drawing attention to ways in which word-groupings may be categorized, used and evaluated. It is hoped that the discussion will not only stimulate interest that could lead to productive research into the subject, but also help teachers to make sensible 'cost-effective' decisions in the very practical matter of allocating classroom time to the teaching of groupings.

2. Grouping Principles

Every Teeline writer knows that single-word outlines are derived by applying certain principles to handwriting, and that learning those principles is the essential first step towards their effective application. It is equally important to understand the principles on which word-groupings are based, for without that knowledge it is virtually impossible to use them extensively, to devise worthwhile groupings, or, indeed, to reach the ultimate objective of being able to write and read them without hesitation.

The joining of two or more full outlines

to be ...., it should be ...., fresh start ....,

passing motorist ...., come forward ....,

at bay ...., used by ...., there are ....,

red light ....

Omissions

(a) A barely or lightly sounded letter, often T or D

I am pleased to say ...., last week ....,

next step ...., great deal ....,

quite true ....

(b) A repeated consonant

Many of these may also qualify as lightly sounded letters:

annual leave ...., better results ....,

as soon as ...., home market ....,

class struggle ...., last time ....

Teeline Word Groupings

(c) A syllable or syllables whose presence is implied by the context

These are often common word beginnings or endings:

due *consideration* ...., motor *industry* ....,

executive committee ...., come to the *conclusion* ....,

isolation ward ...., *invisible* trade ....,

positive reaction ....

(d) A word or words whose presence is implied by the context

These are usually small common words acting as conjunctions, prepositions, adverbs, adjectives or pronouns, and/or the definite or indefinite article. Such groupings require the strong context provided by hackneyed phrases, clichés and other familiar linguistic expressions.

this and that ...., as a rule ...., at the moment ....,

on behalf of ...., more or less ....,

larger and larger ...., with reference to ....,

members of the committee ...., last but not least ....,

sister-in-law ...., spanner in the works ....,

sign of the times ....

The general principle of omission may, at the discretion of the writer, be extended to any letter or letters whose absence does not reduce the readability of a grouping. The alphabetical list in Part Two contains many examples, including:

go away ...., good heavens ....,

carbon copy ....

Positioning

A grouping that contains a word such as *after, above* or *over*, can sometimes be written in such a way that the position of one part of the outline in relation to another part indicates the presence of that word and/or another word, making its inclusion unnecessary.

all over the country ...., above the law ....,

time after time ...., one thing after another ....

3. Groupings Omitted from the Alphabetical List

Using very common words

A large number of frequently occurring word-groupings can be formed from two or more of these words:

I	you	it	we	they	there	that	am	is	are	was
were	will	shall	can	could	should	would	does			
do	did	done	has	have	had	may	might	must		
be	been	seem	seems	seemed	not					

In the main, such groupings have been left out of the alphabetical list for reasons of economy although some of them do appear as part of other groupings such as 'it is possible', 'I would like to say', 'we are sorry' and 'it seems to me'.

It is strongly recommended that students study the above list and construct their own preferred groupings, in most cases simply by joining words together. There are literally hundreds of possibilities, ranging from simple two-word groupings like 'I am', 'there are' and 'has been' to 'it could not be done' and 'that there does not seem to have been'. Finally, when devising their outlines, students should bear in mind that several of the listed words can be written in more than one acceptable way, e.g.:

I (...*K*... or ...*L*...), there (...*V*... or ....), would (...⌐... or ...⌣...),

be/been (...*6*... or ...*Q*...), not (...⌐... or ...⌐...).

Joining ING to UP and DOWN

Numerous groupings can be formed by writing ING ...../...... upwards and

joining UP .....ʏ.....; or downwards and joining DOWN ...⌣...:

coming up ...ᏟᏏ......., coming down .Ꮯᴌᴗ...., doing up ..ᴍᏏ........,

running down ./ᴌᴗ......, looking up ...Ꮯᴍ......., settling down .ᘔᴌᴗ......,

washing up ..⌐�....., bringing up .Ꮾᴷᴹ......, tearing down ....,

letting down ...Ꮯᴌᴗ..., tying up ....ᴷ........., flinging down ..Ꮯᴌᴗ...

10

Using numbers

The following outlines can be extensively used in word-groupings:

hundred .~~~... (written under the preceding figure: 400 ...4......).

thousand .... (written over the preceding figure: 8,000 ....8......).

million ...~..... (written under the preceding figure: 9,000,000 .....9.....).

Examples of groupings

hundred thousand ....~~~..........   five hundred thousand ...5........~..........

hundreds and thousands ....~~~~.~.....   hundreds of ....~~~~~.~.................

hundreds of people ....~~~..........   hundreds of thousands ...~~~~~.~.......

hundred million ....~~~~.~..........   two hundred million
       (200,000,000) ....2.......~..........

hundreds of millions .....~~~.~..........   thousand million ....

eight thousand million   thousands of ....
  (8,000,000,000) ....8.............

thousands of pounds ....~............   thousands of millions ....

millions of...............~~.....................   millions of miles ....~~~.~...............

4. Guide to Alternative Strategies and Outlines

There are few words or word-groupings for which there is only one valid Teeline outline. From the earliest lesson there is an element of choice which, with the guidance of a good teacher or textbook, can be exercised to advantage by any student.

While the classroom teacher may—and should—find time to discuss alternative outlines, authors of textbooks are often subject to the constraints of space and may have to be content with writing only one recommended outline. However, word-groupings offer so much scope for alternatives that it was considered advisable and worthwhile to include them in this book: consequently, two or more outlines are given for many of the groupings in Part Two. Also, as the book is primarily intended for post-theory students, the opportunity has been taken to introduce some alternative strategies and to suggest ways in which those previously published may be extended. It should be noted that these are not untested ideas: they have all been taught on Teeline courses over a number of years and been favourably received and used by a large proportion of the students.

Where appropriate, each of the entries below is followed by at least one example of its application in a word-grouping. In many cases a brief explanatory note is also given.

ADV ....   advisory capacity .... More controllable at

high speed than ....

afternoon ....   Sunday afternoon .... An alternative to

....

-ANGE ....   very strange .... An alternative to

....

-ANK ....   bank statement .... An alternative to

.... Its use may be extended to *bank* as the

last word of a grouping: river bank ....

audio	audio-typist	
authority	my authority .... Written in T-position and detached from preceding word.	
ball	start the ball rolling	
beyond	beyond question	
centre	in the centre ...., music centre	

.... Written through the *centre* of a preceding letter or word.

city	city centre ...., city streets ....

An alternative to detached ....

civic	civic duty ....
civil	civil rights ....
CM	much importance .... An alternative to

.... Especially useful in writing the letter

sequences DCM ...., MCM ....,

OCM ...., QCM ...., RCM

................, TCM ...., VCM

................, WCM ....

CMF	in comfort .... or ....
CMN	in common .... or ....

commercial ....⌇........ commercial training ..⌇............. . The word-ending
-SHL is joined to the CM, giving a speed increase.
Used only as the first word of a grouping.

computer ....⌐........... home computer .....⌐............ . Not used as the first
word of a grouping.

dot ....•............... on the dot ....⌐........... . This may also be used for
spot or *point* in groupings where no ambiguity is

possible: accident black spot ....✗•..........., case in

point ....⌐.......... or ....⌐•......... . N.B. on the

spot ....⌐........., man on the spot ......⌐........ .

down ....⌣............ down in the dumps ..⌣⌐....... . Used only as the

first word of a grouping. As the last word of a

grouping *down* may be written ....⌐.........: come

down .....⌐........ .

end ....⌐............... at the end ....↙........... . Written at the **end** of—and

detached from—the immediately preceding word.

-ENGTH ....⌐............ full strength ....⌐⌐....... . This may also be used for

length: at great length ....⌐.......... . Detached from
preceding letter or word.

EV- ....⌄............... even more ..⌄........ . A more controllable and

readable alternative to ....⌄........... or ....⌄..........

or ....⌄......... .

evening ....⌄............ this evening ....⌐........ .

evidence ....⌄............ circumstantial evidence ....⌐....... . Detached
from preceding letter and written in D-position.

final .... final dividend .... Used only as the first word of a grouping.

financial .... financial reward .... Used only as the first word of a grouping.

Friday .... Friday next ...., Friday evening ....

hand .... hand-made ...., at hand .... Written with the same slope as the A-indicator to show HA. May be joined to or detached from the preceding or following word.

insurance .... car insurance .... An alternative to .... Not used as the first word of a grouping.

intention .... my intention .... Detached from the preceding word and written in the T-position.

large .... at large ...., very large ....

LF .... life and limb .... An alternative to ....

likely .... it is likely .... Used to distinguish *likely* from *lucky* .... and *luckily* ....

long .... before long .... Detached from preceding word.

manager .... bank manager .... A safer abbreviation of MNGR .... than MN ...., avoiding possible confusion with the word *man*.

Teeline Word Groupings

middle .... ⌢ .... in the middle .... ⌤ .... Written through the
middle of a preceding letter or word.

-MND .... ⌢ .... in demand .... ⌤ .... Detached and written in D-

position. Not used to begin a grouping.

MNT .... ⌢ .... in mint condition .... ⌤⌐ .... An extended use of
the word-ending -MENT.

Monday .... ⌢ .... next Monday .... ⌢ ....

morning .... ⌢ .... Monday morning ⌢ ⌐ ,...., this morning

... ⌐ ....

on .... ⌐ .... on a shoestring ... ⌐ .... A join of .... ⌐ ....

and .... ⌐ .... which greatly reduces the

possibility of misreading the ON blend .... ⌐ ....

as the letter Y .... ⌐ ...., and vice versa.

on the .... ⌐ .... on the carpet .... ⌐ .... Used as the first two

words of a grouping, detached and written above the
following letter or word.

once .... ⌐ .... once more .... ⌐ .... Used as the first word of a
grouping, detached and written above the following
letter or word.

opinion .... / .... in my opinion .... ⌐ ...., I am of the opinion

.... ⌐ .... The letter P written with the same

slope as the I-indicator to show PI. Written through a
preceding letter or word.

out of .... ⌣ .... out of step .... ⌐ ....

over .... ⌣ .... annual turnover .... ⌐ .... An alternative to the

16

word-ending ....✓.......... . Written **over** the last word or letter of a grouping.

QR ....✓............. square peg ....✓........ . An alternative to ....✓.......... . The letter Q is sloped to allow this letter sequence to be written in one movement.

racial ....✓............. racial tension ....✓.......... . The word-ending -SHL is joined to the R, giving a speed increase. Used only as the first word of a grouping.

Saturday ....✓............. Saturday afternoon ...✓.................. .

sentence .... light sentence ......✓.......... . Detached from the preceding word and written in the T-position.

ship/ ....S................ shipping ship building ....S✓........., shipping industry S✓........ . Disjoined SH as first word of a grouping.

short .... short cut ....✓........... . Chiefly used as the first word of a grouping but may be used as the last word when unambiguous: cut short ....

social ....✓............. social worker ...✓........✓...... . The word-ending -SHL is joined to the S giving a speed increase. Used only as the first word of a grouping.

soft C ....✓............. very nice ....✓.......... . Used as an alternative to ....✓......... only when the letter C is pronounced S and when ....✓.......... improves the readability or fluency of the grouping.

Sunday ....✓............. next Sunday ....✓.......... .

these ....✓............. these days ....✓........ . Written with a perpendicular H (the same slope as the E-indicator)

17

to show TH*E*S. Note also *this* ......✓............ (I-indicator slope) and *those* ....╲........ (includes O-indicator).

thing ....✓............

next thing ....✗........ . An extension of the word-ending -ING.

think ....✓............

I can think ....✓......... . An alternative to

.........✓......... . Not used as the first word of a grouping.

thinking ....✗............

good thinking ....✗............ . Not used as the first word of a grouping.

Thursday ....✓............

Thursday evening .....✗........... .

top ....

top drawer ⌣........ . Written above (on **top** of) the following letter or word. Used only as the first word of a grouping.

Tuesday ....✗............

Tuesday evening ....✗............ .

UN- ....✗............

unanimous decision ..✗........ . An alternative to

...........✗......... . Written to distinguish the pronunciation of UN (unit, unilateral) from UN (until, unable). An aid to fluent and accurate note-reading and transcription.

Wednesday ......✗.........

next Wednesday ...✗........... .

where ....

where the ....✗...... . An alternative to

..........✗........... . As the first word of a grouping it is written in the T-position.

world ....✗.........

world trade ✗......✗.... . Usually detached in D-position, but may be joined to preceding or following letter if remaining readable: it is a small world

.....✗........, worlds apart ....✗........ .

5. Teewords

A Teeword is simply an artificial 'word' invented as a memory aid for a word-grouping. By means of a Teeword even a multi-word grouping may be easily memorized, thus helping the writer to achieve the ultimate objective of writing the outline as fluently as if it were indeed a single word. The most effective Teewords are those devised by the individual writer for his or her own use: the main purpose of the following list is to demonstrate the scope of this idea.

Grouping	Teeword	Outline
Act of Parliament	actparl	
annual election	anlec	
annual leave	anleave	
annual meeting	anming	
annual occasion	ancasion	
annual profit	anpof	
annual rent	anrent	
annual report	anrep	
annual report and accounts	anrepacs	
annual report and balance sheet	anrebalsheet	
annual return	anreturn	
annual review	anrev	
annual statement	anstament	

19

Grouping	Teeword	Outline
annual subscription	ansub	
annual trade	antrade	
annual trade deficit	antradef	
annual trade surplus	antradesurp	
as a last resort	aslastresor	
as a matter of course	asmattercourse	
as a matter of fact	asmatteract	
as a matter of form	asmatterform	
as a matter of interest	asmatteriterest	
as a matter of trust	asmattertrust	
as a matter of urgency	asmattergy	
assaulting a police officer	assaulpofficer	
at sixes and sevens	atsixevens	
balance of credit	balcred	
balance of payments	bapments	
balance of payments deficit	bapmentsdef	
balance of payments surplus	bapmentsurp	
balance of stock	balstock	

Grouping	Teeword	Outline
balance of trade	baltrade	
balance sheet	balsheet	
bargain basement	bargasement	
bargain hunter	bargunter	
bargain hunting	bargunting	
bill of exchange	billex	
both sides of industry	bosindy	
bound over	bover	
bound over in the sum of	boversum	
bound over to keep the peace	boverpeace	
by no means	bynomes	
can be expected	canbex	
captains of industry	capsindy	
car insurance	carsurance	
civil disobedience	civdis	
civil liberty	civlib	
civil rights	civrights	
civil servant	civsernt	

Grouping	Teeword	Outline
civil service	civserve	
civil tongue	civtong	
college of technology	coltec	
comparability study	compasty	
compassionate leave	compleave	
conventional weapons	convepons	
cool, calm and collected	coocamcol	
corporal punishment	corpushment	
corporation tax	corporax	
cost of living	costling	
criminal act	crimalact	
criminal negligence	crimalgence	
criminal violence	crimalence	
cumulative preference shares	cumpreshares	
damaged beyond repair	dambrepair	
declare a dividend	decladiv	
demarcation dispute	demardis	
discount for cash	discash	
discount market	discmar	

22

Grouping	Teeword	Outline
false economy	falsecon	
fatal accident	fatalax	
free collective bargaining	freecobing	
government expenditure	gex or govex	
government intervention	govention	
government minister	gominister or govinister	
government spending	gosping or govsping	
guest of honour	gestonour	
happy-go-lucky	haplucky	
his and hers	hisaners	
home computer	homeputer	
how many	homany	
hustle and bustle	husbusle	
immediate action	immedaction	
important area	impara	
in part exchange	inparex	
income tax	icomax	
industrial action	idustraction	

23

Teeline Word Groupings

Grouping	Teeword	Outline
industrial dispute	idustrispute	
industrial relations	idustrations	
interim dividend	iterimdiv or iterdiv	
it goes without saying	itgosaying	
kill or cure	kilcure	
kingdom come	kingcom	
law and order	lawder	
leaders of industry	leadersindy	
local productivity agreement	locprodment	
local productivity deal	locprodel	
low productivity	lowprody	
majority verdict	majver	
motor accident	motorax	
motor car accident	motorcarax	
multilateral disarmament	multilaterdis	
needless to say	needlesay	
no-go area	nogora	

Grouping	Teeword	Outline
odds and ends	oddsends	
optical illusion	oplusion	
overdraft facilities	overdrafilities	
personal computer	persputer	
police officer	pofficer	
police station	polstation	
post-mortem examination	posmorex	
present company excepted	prescomex	
prices and incomes policy	pricompol	
productivity deal	prodel	
profit and loss account	proflossac	
public servant	pubsernt	
public service	pubserve	
question time	questime	
rarefied atmosphere	rarefatmos	
raw materials	rawterials	
read and adopted	redopted	

Teeline Word Groupings

Grouping	Teeword	Outline
redeemable preference shares	represhares	
report and accounts	repacs	
restrictive practices	restractices	
school-leaver	scolver	
school-leaving age	scolvage	
secondary picketing	spicketing	
selective strike action	selstraction	
self-financing productivity deal	selprodel	
separate rooms	seprooms	
serious accident	serisax	
slower and slower	slowower	
standard of living	stanling or stalving	
strike action	straction	
telephone bill	telbill	
telephone call	telcall	
telephone conversation	telcon	
to a large extent	tolarex	
to an extent	tonex	

Grouping	Teeword	Outline
to some extent	tosmex	
trials and tribulations	trialstribs	
up to the minute	upmin	
upside down	upsidown	
utter rubbish	utterbish	
utterly ridiculous	utteridic	
valuable asset	valasset	
vast area	vastara	
victim of circumstance	victcirc	
visible earnings	visernings	
vital statistics	vitstics	
with all due respect	waldresp	
with regard to	wigar	
work-to-rule	worktrule	

Part Two
6. Alphabetical List of Groupings

All the listed groupings derive from the principles identified in Part One, and each one has the potential to increase writing speed. Outlines differing from those appearing in other Teeline publications should be regarded as alternatives. Where two or more outlines are given for one grouping, these also should be regarded as alternatives.

a

a lot of people

a lot of things

a number of things

a question of time

a step in the right direction

about it

about that

about that time

about the

about these

about this

about those

about time

about which

above all

above average

above-board

above criticism

above-mentioned

above par

above reproach

above suspicion

above the

above the law

absent without leave

absolute discharge

accident black spot

accident black spots

accident insurance

accident prevention

accident-prone

accident report form

accident ward

accidental death

31

account for ....

accounted for ....

acquired taste ....

across the ....

across the board ....

across the country ....

across the road ....

across the street ....

across the world ....

Act of Parliament ....

action stations ....

added expense ....

added to the ....

additional expenditure ....

additional expense ....

admissible evidence ....

advisory capacity ....

advisory committee ....

after all ....

after-sales service ....

after that ....

after the ....

again and again ....

age of consent ....

age of reason ....

air and sea ....

air-conditioning ....

all about it ....

all along ....

all and sundry ....

all around the world ....

all at once ....

all circumstances ....

all day long ....

all eventualities ....

all in a day's work ....

all in all ....

all in good time ....

all kinds ....

all kinds of ....

all of a sudden ....

all of us ....

all of you

all over again

all over the country

all over the world

all parts of the world

all people

all possibilities

all right

all round the world

all sorts

all sorts of

all sorts of things

all that

all the

all the best

all the circumstances

all the same

all the time

all things

all things considered

all told

all very well

all well and good

all wrong

alleged offence

almost impossible

along the

alphabetical order

among the

and so forth

and so on

and the

annual election

annual general meeting

annual leave

annual meeting

annual occasion

annual profit

annual rent

annual report

annual report and
accounts

33

annual report and
balance sheet ....

annual return ....

annual review ....

annual statement ....

annual subscription ....

annual trade ....

annual trade deficit ....

annual trade surplus ....

annual turnover ....

another part ....

another thing ....

any bank ....

any more than ....

anywhere else ....

application form ....

are you ....

are you quite sure ....

are you sure ....

around the ....

around the clock ....

around the world ....

as a last resort ....

as a matter of course ....

as a matter of fact ....

as a matter of form ....

as a matter of interest ....

as a matter of trust ....

as a matter of urgency ....

as a result ....

as a whole ....

as an example ....

as bad as ....

as compared to ....

as compared with ....

as far as ....

as far as I am concerned ....

as far as possible ....

as good as ....

as great as ....

as I have ....

as I have said ....

as I said

as I say

as if

as is

as it was

as it were

as large as

as large as life

as long as

as long as possible

as much as

as much as possible

as small as

as soon as

as soon as possible

as that

as the

as though

as to

as was

as well

as well as

assaulting a police
  officer

assistant manager

at all

at any cost

at any price

at any rate

at any time

at Christmas

at close quarters

at cross purposes

at first

at first hand

at first sight

at great expense

at great length

at hand

at home

at home and abroad

at large

at last

at last ....

at least ....

at leisure ....

at length ....

at liberty ....

at loggerheads ....

at long last ....

at most ....

at night ....

at no time ....

at once ....

at peace ....

at present ....

at rest ....

at sixes and sevens ....

at some length ....

at some point ....

at some stage ....

at some time ....

at some time or other ....

at the beginning ....

36

at that ....

at that moment ....

at that moment in time ....

at that point ....

at that point in time ....

at that stage ....

at that time ....

at the ....

at the beginning ....

at the best of times ....

at the double ....

at the end ....

at the end of the day ....

at the end of the month ....

at the end of the week ....

at the end of the year ....

at the moment ....

at the most ....

at the other extreme ....

at the present moment ....

at the present moment in time ....

at the present time ......

at the same place ....

at the same rate ......

at the same time ....

at the start ....

at the time ....

at the top ....

at this moment ....

at this moment in time ....

at this point ....

at this point in time ....

at this stage ....

at this time ....

at your earliest convenience ....

atom bomb ....

atomic bomb ......

atomic energy ....

atomic fuel ....

atomic pile ....

atomic power ....

atomic waste ....

audio-typing ....

audio-typist ....

audio-visual ....

average earnings ....

average price ....

average turnover ....

aware of the fact ....

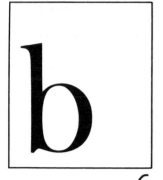

back number

back seat

back to back

back to front

backward and forward

backwards and forwards

bad accident

bad books

bad language

bad luck

bad manners

bad thing

bad to worse

baggage allowance

balance due

balance of credit

balance of payments

balance of payments deficit

balance of payments surplus

balance of stock

balance of trade

balance sheet

bank account

bank lending

bank manager

bank mortgage

bank overdraft

bank rate

bank statement

banker's order

bare essentials

bargain basement

bargain hunter

bargain hunting

be-all and end-all

be there/their

bear in mind ....

bearing in mind ....

beat/beating about the
   bush ....

before long ....

before that ....

before the ....

before the court ....

before us ....

before very long ....

before you ....

beginning to rain ....

beginning to see ....

beginning to think ....

behind the scenes ....

behind the times ....

believe it or not ....

below par ....

benefit of the doubt ....

beside the point ....

best attention ....

best buy ....

best efforts ....

best interests ....

best man ....

best offer ....

best of all worlds ....

best of both worlds ....

best of luck ....

best of my ability ....

best of our ability ....

best regards ....

best results ....

best terms ....

best thing ....

best view ....

best way ....

best wishes ....

better late than never ....

better off ....

better results ....

better than ....

better than ever		blank cheque	
between ourselves		blood pressure	
between themselves		blood transfusion	
beyond a joke		board of directors	
beyond doubt		body and soul	
beyond question		bonus issue	
beyond reach		born and bred	
beyond recall		borne in mind	
big bank		borough council	
big business		borough councillor	
bigger than		borough surveyor	
bill of exchange		both sides of industry	
bill of fare		bound over	
birth control		bound over in the sum of	
bit by bit		bound over to keep the peace	
bit less		boys will be boys	
bit more		brain drain	
bitter end		branch manager	
bitter pill		branch office	
black spot		breach of the peace	
black spots			

bread and butter	bus station
breaking and entering	bus ticket
breath test	business computer
breathing-space	business deal
bright idea	business expenses
bright spark	business investment
bring forward	business letter
British industry	business matter
broad agreement	business studies
broad area	by accident
broadly speaking	by all accounts
brought about	by all means
brought back	by and by
brought forward	by and large
brother and sister	by any means
brother-in-law	by no means
budget account	by post
building industry	by-product
building society	by return post
bus driver	by the
bus service	by the end

by the end of the day

by the end of the day ...⟋ ...⟋ ....

by the end of the month ...⟋ ...⟋ ......

by the end of the week ...⟋ ...⟋ .....

by the end of the year ...⟋ ...⟋ ....

by the time ...⟋ ....

by the way ....⟋ ....

42

C

call/called a meeting

call/called back

call/called down

call/called for

call/called in

call/called it a day

call/called me back

call/called off

call/called out

call/called to mind

call/called up

came/come away

came/come back

came/come by

came/come clean

came/come down

came/come down in the world

came/come down to earth

came/come for

came/come forward

came/come from

came/come full circle

came/come straight to the point

came/come to grief

came/come to life

came/come to nothing

came/come to terms

came/come to the conclusion

came/come to the crunch

came/come to the point

came/come unstuck

came/come up

came/come up in the world

can be expected

can say

43

can you

can you	carry on
can you say	carry over
capital costs	case dismissed
capital expenditure	case in point
capital investment	cash discount
capital of the company	cash dispenser
capital punishment	cash in hand
capital requirements	cash on delivery
capital sum	cash with order
captains of industry	cassette recorder
car accident	caught in the act
car crash	caught red-handed
car driver	cause of the accident
car insurance	Central Criminal Court
car-park	certificate of insurance
car racing	chairman and managing director
carbon copy	chairman of the board
cardiac arrest	chairman of the committee
cardiac massage	chairman of the company
careful consideration	chairman of the council
carry/carried forward	

44

Chamber of Commerce	citizen's arrest
Chamber of Trade	civic centre
Chancellor of the Exchequer	civic duty
change gear	civil disobedience
change hands	civil liberty
change of address	civil rights
change partners	civil servant
character reference	civil service
charged with	civil tongue
chartered accountant	claim for compensation
chartered surveyor	class interests
circulated statement	class struggle
circumstantial evidence	class system
city centre	class warfare
city council	classic example
city councillor	clean break
city hall	clean hands
City of London	clean sweep
city streets	clean up
city transport	clear up
	close connection

close contest

close contest

close down

close encounter

close examination

close quarters

close relationship

close shave

close thing

close up

closed shop

closed up

closer examination

closing date

coast to coast

code of practice

cold storage

cold store

cold sweat

college of technology

coming and going

coming week

coming year

comings and goings

commercial agreement

commercial break

commercial department

commercial development

commercial division

commercial insurance

commercial investment

commercial manager

commercial markets

commercial network

commercial practice

commercial premises

commercial property

commercial radio

commercial stations

commercial television

commercial trade

commercial training

commercial transaction

commercial TV

comprehensive insurance

commercial undertaking

comprehensive policy

commercial venture

compulsory purchase

commercial work

compulsory purchase order

commercial world

computer game

committee member

computer programmer

commodity market

computer terminal

common enemy

conditional discharge

common ground

conditions of service

Common Market

conference decision

common or garden

confidential information

common sense

confidential matter

common touch

confidential report

community centre

consider/considered to be

company car

construction industry

company chairman

company secretary

consultative document

comparability study

consumer affairs

compassionate leave

consumer research

complete agreement

container ship

contradictory evidence

47

conventional weapons

conventional weapons ....

conventional wisdom ....

convincing argument ....

cool, calm and collected ....

corporal punishment ....

corporation tax ....

cost of living ....

could you ....

council chamber ....

council member ....

counsel for the defence ....

counsel for the
prosecution ....

count the cost ....

countries in the
world ....

countries of the
world ....

county council ....

county hall ....

county surveyor ....

Court of Appeal ....

court order ....

court reporter ....

court reporting ....

cover/covered up ....

credit account ....

credit card ....

credit facilities ....

credit squeeze ....

credit transfer ....

crime sheet ....

criminal act ....

criminal negligence ....

criminal violence ....

cross-examination ....

cross-purposes ....

cross-section ....

crossed warrant ....

crystal clear ....

cumulative preference
shares ....

cup of tea ....

48

current account ....

current account deficit .....

current account surplus ....

current year ....

custom-built ....

customer services ....

cut across ....

cut and dried ....

cut away ....

cut back ....

cut corners ....

cut costs ....

cut down ....

cut free ....

cut off ....

cut out ....

cut production costs ....

cut short ....

cut up ....

49

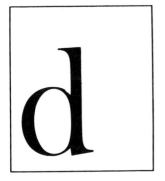

damaged beyond repair

dangerous driving

dangerous precedent

dangerous step

data processing

day after day

day after tomorrow

day and night

day before yesterday

day by day

day in, day out

day of the week

daylight robbery

days of the week

days on end

dead and buried

dead and gone

dead end

dead loss

dead to the world

Dear Madam

Dear Miss

Dear Mr

Dear Mrs

Dear Ms

Dear Sir

Dear Sirs

Dear Sir or Madam

death from natural causes

debenture holder

debenture issue

debit account

declare a dividend

deep trouble

defence counsel

delivered to you ....

delivery date ....

demarcation dispute ....

deposit account ....

deputy chairman ....

development area ....

development plan ....

different from ....

directors' report ....

dirty look ....

dirty story ....

dirty trick ....

dirty work ....

discount for cash ....

discount market ....

disc drive ....

disqualified from driving ....

district council ....

documentary evidence ....

dog-tired ....

domestic policy ....

donkey-work ....

donkey's years ....

do's and don'ts ....

dot matrix ....

dot matrix printer ....

double Dutch ....

down-and-out ....

down the drain ....

down-to-earth ....

down tools ....

draft agreement ....

draft contract ....

drastic measures ....

draw attention ....

draw/drew my attention ....

draw/drew your attention ....

dried up ....

drink and drive ....

drinking and driving ....

driving lesson ....

driving-licence ....

driving seat

driving seat .... ⟋ ....

driving test .... ⟋ ....

driving without
  a licence .....⟋⟍ ....

driving without due care
  and attention .....⟋⟍ ....

drug addict .... ⟋⟍ ....

drug addiction .... ⟋⟍ ....

drug offences .... ⟋⟍ ....

drunk and incapable ....⟋⟍ ...⟋⟍ .

due consideration ....⟋⟍ ....

during last month ....⟋⟍ ....⟋⟍ .

during last week ....⟋⟍ ....⟋⟍ ...

during last year .... ⟋⟍ ....

during next month ....⟋⟍ ....⟋⟍ .

during next week .....⟋⟍ .....⟋⟍ .

during next year .... ⟋⟍ ....

during recent months ...⟋⟍ ...⟋⟍ .

during recent weeks ...⟋⟍ ....⟋⟍ .

during recent years ....⟋⟍ ....

during the coming
  month ....⟋⟍ ...⟋⟍ ....

during the coming
  week ....⟋⟍ ...⟋⟍ ....

during the coming year ....⟋⟍ ......

during the course of .....⟋⟍ .....

during the day ....⟋⟍ ....

during the last
  month ....⟋⟍ ......⟋⟍ ...

during the last
  week ....⟋⟍ .....⟋⟍ .....

during the last year ....⟋⟍ ....

during the month ....⟋⟍ ....⟋⟍ .

during the next
  month ....⟋⟍ ....⟋⟍ ...

during the next
  week ....⟋⟍ .....⟋⟍ ...

during the next year ....⟋⟍ ....

during the past month ...⟋⟍ ...⟋⟍ ....

during the past week ...⟋⟍ ....⟋⟍ ...

during the past year ......⟋⟍ ....

during the previous
  month ......⟋⟍ .....⟋⟍ ...

during the previous
  week ....⟋⟍ .....⟋⟍ ....

during the previous year ....⟋⟍ .....

during their stay

during the week ....~~~~.~~c........   during their ....~~~~.←~~~..............

during the year ....——~u..............   during their stay ...~~~~~:⟋~~~.~~.........

during the year under
  review ....——.u⤳..........

53

each and every ....

each and every one ....

each day ....

each end ....

each kind ....

each month ....

each of them ....

each of us ....

each of you ....

each one ....

each other ....

each sort ....

each thing ....

each time ....

each type ....

each way ....

each week ....

each year ....

earliest convenience ....

early reply ....

easier said than done ....

east coast ....

east to west ....

easy come easy go ....

easy on the eye ....

economic forecast ....

economic policy ....

economic strategy ....

economy of the country ....

education committee ....

electric typewriter ....

electronic mail ....

electronic typewriter ....

emergency measures ....

encouraging trend ....

end of the day ....

end of the month ....

end of the quarter ....

end of the road ....

end of the week ....

end of the year ....

end-product ....

end result ....

end to end ....

end up ....

entered a plea of guilty ....

entered a plea of not
guilty ....

entertainment
centre ....

equal opportunities ....

equal pay ....

equal rights ....

equal shares ....

equity capital ....

error of judgement ....

estimated cost ....

eternal triangle ....

even if ....

even more .....

even so ....

even though ....

ever after ....

ever-increasing ....

ever more ....

ever-popular ....

ever-present ....

ever-rising ....

ever since ....

every day ....

every minute ....

every month .....

every second ....

every so often ....

every time ....

every way ....

every week ....

every year ....

exact words ....

exceptional circumstances ....

exchange rate

exchange rate ....

executive committee ....

executive decision ....

executive officer ....

executive position ....

expert evidence ....

expert opinion ....

expert witness ....

expert witnesses ....

export business ....

export company ....

export manager ....

export markets ....

export sales ....

extra charge ....

extra hours ....

extra income ....

extra large ....

extramarital ....

extra-mural ....

extra payment ....

extra special ....

extra time ....

extra value ....

extra work ....

extraordinary general
meeting ....

56

face the music

face to face

face up

face up to things

face value

fact of life

facts of life

fair and square

fair deal

fair game

fair hair

fair play

fairly and squarely

fall away

fall down

fall in

fall off

fall out

false alarm

false economy

false start

false teeth

family life

family matter

far above

far and wide

far away

far cry

far cry from

far distant

far enough

far from

far from it

far off

farther on

farther than

fast and furious

fast and loose

fast and loose ....

faster and faster ....

fatal accident ....

fatal error ....

fatal mistake ....

father-in-law ....

fed up ....

few days ....

few days ago ....

few days' time ....

few minutes ....

few minutes ago ....

few minutes' time ....

few months ....

few months ago ....

few months'
  time ....

few of them ....

few of us ....

few of you ....

few people ....

58

few things ....

few times ....

few ways ....

few weeks ....

few weeks ago ....

few weeks'
  time ....

few words ....

few years ....

few years ago ....

few years' time ....

fewer and fewer ....

field-day ....

field sports ....

final decision ....

final dividend ....

final report ....

finance committee ....

financial crises ....

financial crisis ....

financial difficulties ....

financial gain	first-class
financial problems	first half
financial report	first of all
financial restraint	first offence
financial restrictions	first offender
financial reward	first offer
financial statement	first person
financial troubles	first-rate
fire-alarm	first refusal
fire brigade	first thing
fire insurance	first time
fire officer	first witness
fire precautions	fishing industry
fire service	flexi-time
firm conviction	floppy disc
firm decision	flow of traffic
firm denial	flying start
firm intention	follow on
firm offer	follow suit
first and foremost	follow up
first base	fool's errand

59

football ground

football ground

for a

for a long time

for a moment

for a short time

for a start

for a very long time

for a very short time

for a while

for all time

for and against

for better or worse

for dear life

for ever

for ever and ever

for evermore

for example

for export

for goodness' sake

for instance

for old times' sake

for sale

for some time

for that

for that matter

for that reason

for the

for the first time

for the last time

for the moment

for the most part

for the present moment

for the time being

for these reasons

for this reason

for those reasons

foreign language

foreign trade

forensic evidence

forensic science

found guilty

found not guilty	from side to side
frankly speaking	from start to finish
free and easy	from strength to strength
free collective bargaining	from that moment
free delivery	from that moment in time
free gift	from the
free kick	from the beginning
free of charge	from the first
free speech	from the start
freedom of speech	from time immemorial
freedom of the press	from time to time
fresh start	front seat
Friday afternoon	frozen assets
Friday evening	full authority
Friday morning	full employment
Friday next	full enquiry
Friday night	full extent
from beginning to end	full length
from day to day	full marks
from end to end	full measure
from first to last	full of beans

61

full of joy

full of joy ....

full order book ....

full recovery ....

full stop ....

full strength ....

full support ....

full time ....

full-time course ....

full-time education ....

full-time employment ....

full-time job ....

full up ....

fully comprehensive
  insurance ....

fully fit ....

fully occupied ....

fully recovered ....

fun and games ....

furniture and fittings ....

further action ....

further and further ....

further consideration ....

further evidence ....

further information ....

further inquiries ....

further on ....

further than ....

future actions ....

future conduct ....

future occasion ....

future reference ....

future years ....

g

garden centre

garden party

garden path

gave/give evidence

gave/give up

gave/give way

general election

general manager

general public

general purposes
committee

general reserve

generally speaking

get/got about

get/got away

get/got back

get/got beaten

get/got better

get/got cracking

get/got down

get/got forward

get/got from

get/got in

get/got inside

get/got lost

get/got more than

get/got moving

get/got nothing

get/got off

get/got on

get/got out

get/got together

get/got up

get/got working

ghost writer

gin and tonic

give and take

glad to be

glad to say

glad to see

go away

go back

go down

go forward

go on

go together

gone away

good behaviour

good boss

good business

good company

good deal

good enough

good example

good-for-nothing

good fun

good health

good heavens

good intentions

good life

good luck

good manners

good meal

good measure

good name

good old days

good people

good question

good reason

good relations

good relationship

good result

good riddance

good sense

good show

good sort

good start

good story

good terms

good thing

good thinking

good time

good turn

good wishes

goods and services

goods in transit

government expenditure

government intervention

government minister

government policy

government spending

grand total

grass roots

great advance

great advantage

Great Britain

great deal

great effort

great idea

great importance

great improvement

great many

great need

great performance

great regret

great respect

great response

great responsibility

great satisfaction

great stuff

great surprise

great thing

great value

greater and greater

greater than

ground-rent

ground rules

guest of honour

guest speaker

guide-dog

65

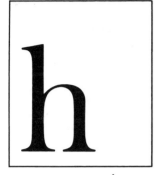

had gone

half a mile

half an hour

half and half

half-hearted

half-hour

half-mile

half-time

half-way

hammer and tongs

hand in glove

hand in hand

handmade

hand over fist

hand over hand

hand-picked

hand to hand

hand to mouth

hand weapon

happy-go-lucky

hard- and -fast rule

hard core

hard-hearted

hard life

hard luck

hard of hearing

hard pressed

hard pushed

hard to understand

hard up

hard work

harder than

hardly likely

harsh sentence

head and shoulders

head first

head start

66

heads of departments	his and hers ....
health centre	hit and run .....
health service	hit-and-run driver ....
heart transplant	hit-or-miss ....
heaven-sent	holiday booking ....
heavy expenditure	holiday insurance ....
here and now	home and abroad ....
here and there	home and dry ....
here, there and everywhere	home-baked ....
high and dry	home comforts ....
high and mighty	home computer ....
High Court	home cooking ....
high pressure	home from home ....
high productivity	home-made ....
high proportion	home-made bread ....
high-street shops	home market ....
higher and higher	Home Office ....
higher than	home-produced ....
hire-purchase	Home Secretary ....
hire-purchase payments	home trade ....

home truth

home truth

homeless people

honest answer

Honourable Member

honoured guest

hopping mad

hornets' nest

hospital doctor

hospital insurance

hospital management

hospital nurse

hospital ward

hour after hour

hour by hour

hours ago

house contents insurance

house insurance

House of Commons

House of Lords

House of Representatives

house purchase

house rules

house to house

household name

household word

Houses of Parliament

housing committee

housing department

housing development

housing estate

how far

how many

how much

human being

human error

human race

hunger-strike

hustle and bustle

hydrogen bomb

68

I am pleased to see ....

I am right ....

I am sorry ....

I am sorry to say ....

I am sorry to see ....

I am afraid ....

I am sure ....

I am certain ....

I am thinking ....

I am glad ....

I assure you ....

I am glad to say ....

I believe ....

I am glad to see ....

I can assure you ....

I am going ....

I can say ....

I am not afraid ....

I can see ....

I am not certain ....

I can think ....

I am not right ....

I cannot be sure ....

I am not sorry ....

I cannot say ....

I am not sure ....

I cannot see ....

I am not wrong ....

I cannot think ....

I am of the opinion ....

I consider ....

I am pleased ....

I could not say ....

I am pleased to report ....

I could not see ....

I am pleased to say ....

I could say ....

I could see

I could see	I must see
I dare say	I prefer
I did not say	I presume
I did not see	I propose
I did not think	I refer
I did say	I regret
I did see	I regret to say
I did so	I saw
I did think	I say
I do not doubt	I see
I do not say	I should like
I do not see	I should like to say
I do not think	I should like to see
I do say	I should say
I do see	I should see
I do so	I should think
I do think	I speak
I expect	I suggest
I go	I thank you
I hope	I think
I must say	I think that

70

I trust	if not ....
I try	if there is ....
I venture to suggest	if there is not ....
I was not right	ill at ease ....
I was not wrong	ill-equipped ....
I was quite right	ill-fated ....
I was quite wrong	ill-favoured ....
I was right	ill-feeling ....
I was wrong	ill-mannered ....
I will say	ill-tempered ....
I will see	ill-timed ....
I wish	immediate action ....
I wish to say	immediate attention ....
I wish to see	important appointment ....
I wonder	important area ....
I would like	important case ....
I would like to say	important date ....
I would like to see	important decision ....
I would say	important discussion ....
if and when	important matter ....
if it is possible	important occasion ....

71

important point

important point ....

important question ....

in a bad way ....

in a manner of speaking ....

in a mess ....

in a minute ....

in a moment ....

in a nutshell ....

in a quandary ....

in a second ....

in a vicious circle ....

in a way ....

in abeyance ....

in accordance with ....

in action ....

in addition ....

in advance ....

in agreement ....

in all cases ....

in all conscience ....

in all probability ....

in all respects ....

in all the
wide world ....

in all the world ....

in all things ....

in any case ....

in bed ....

in between ....

in broad daylight ....

in case ....

in certain respects ....

in certain things ....

in certain ways ....

in character ....

in clover ....

in comfort ....

in common ....

in complete agreement ....

in conclusion ....

in confidence ....

in connection with ....

72

in connexion with ....

in consequence ....

in control ....

in custody ....

in danger ....

in debt ....

in deep trouble ....

in default ....

in demand ....

in depth ....

in despair ....

in dire straits ....

in disgrace ....

in disguise ....

in disgust ....

in dispute ....

in doubt ....

in dribs and drabs ....

in due course ....

in effect ....

in error ....

in every way ....

in evidence ....

in excess of ....

in existence ....

in fact ....

in favour ....

in favour of ....

in force ....

in front ....

in front of ....

in full ....

in full agreement ....

in full cry ....

in full flight ....

in full settlement ....

in full view ....

in future ....

in general ....

in good condition ....

in good order ....

in good stead ....

in good time ....

in great need ....

in great pain ....

in hand ....

in judgement ....

in labour ....

in law ....

in lieu ....

in lieu of ....

in love ....

in many cases ....

in many things ....

in many ways ....

in mid-air .....

in mid-stream ....

in mind ....

in mint condition ....

in moderation ....

in most cases ....

in most things ....

in most ways ....

in motion ....

in my opinion ....

in my view ...

in need ....

in next to no time ....

in next to no time at all .....

in no time ....

in no time at all ....

in order ....

in order that ....

in order to ....

in order to do so ......

in order to have ....

in other words ...

in part-exchange ....

in part-payment ....

in particular ....

in passing ....

in payment of account ....

in perfect condition .....

in person

in point ....

in point of fact ....

in practice ....

in preference ....

in preparation ....

in prime condition ....

in prison ....

in production ....

in protest ....

in recent months ....

in recent weeks ....

in recent years ....

in reply ....

in reply to your letter ....

in reserve ....

in response ....

in retrospect ....

in return ....

in season ....

in sequence ....

in serious trouble ....

in-service ....

in-service training ....

in session ....

in several ways ....

in short ....

in simple terms ....

in so many things ....

in so many ways ....

in solitary confinement ....

in solution ....

in some ....

in some cases ....

in some detail ....

in some force ....

in some parts ....

in some quarters ....

in some respects ....

in some sort ....

in some things ....

in some ways ....

in spite of ....

75

in step	in the centre
in stock	in the circumstances
in store	in the city
in such	in the city centre
in such a way	in the corner
in such ways	in the country
in terrible trouble	in the county
in that	in the course of
in that case	in the course of time
in that event	in the dark
in that respect	in the district
in that way	in the dock
in the	in the doldrums
in the afternoon	in the driving seat
in the air	in the end
in the back	in the evening
in the back seat	in the event
in the balance	in the final analysis
in the beginning	in the finish
in the blood	in the fire
in the case	in the first instance

in the road

in the first place

in the flesh

in the front

in the future

in the garage

in the garden

in the interim

in the last analysis

in the last resort

in the long run

in the long term

in the main

in the making

in the market

in the mass

in the matter

in the meantime

in the middle

in the money

in the morning

in the national interest

in the near future

in the next street

in the nick of time

in the north

in the nude

in the offing

in the park

in the passenger seat

in the past

in the past month

in the past week

in the past year

in the picture

in the pink

in the public interest

in the raw

in the rear

in the red

in the right

in the right way

in the road

77

in the running

in the running

in the same boat

in the same place

in the same way

in the second place

in the short run

in the short term

in the south

in the street

in the swim

in the town

in the town centre

in the way

in the words of

in the wrong way

in the year

in the year under review

in theory

in these days

in this day and age

in this matter

in this respect

in this way

in those days

in time

in trouble

in view

in view of

in violation

in which

inadmissible evidence

income and expenditure

income tax

inconclusive evidence

incontrovertible evidence

increased profits

incurable disease

index linked

industrial action

industrial dispute

industrial investment

industrial performance

industrial production

industrial relations

industrial strife

information received

information technology

ins and outs

inside information

inside out

inside story

instead of

insurance adjuster

insurance agent

insurance assessor

insurance broker

insurance claim

insurance company

insurance cover

insurance firm

insurance inspector

insurance man

insurance policy

insurance premium

insurance quotation

insurance salesman

insurance salesmen

intensive care

inter-city service

inter-city train

inter-city transport

interest rate

interesting point

interim dividend

international agreement

international assignment

international co-operation

international exhibition

international trade

into action

into debt

into that

into the

into the matter

into the matter

into these

into this

into those

invisible earnings

invisible trade

Iron Age

Iron Lady

Iron Man

isolated case

isolated incident

isolation hospital

isolation ward

issued capital of the company

it could be possible

it goes

it goes without saying

it is a

it is a good idea

it is a good thing

it is a great idea

it is a great pity

it is a great shame

it is a long time

it is a long time since

it is a long way

it is a long while

it is a miracle

it is a pity

it is a question of

it is a shame

it is a small world

it is a strange thing

it is a terrible thing

it is a tragedy

it is about time

it is all right

it is all very well

it is all well and good

it is all wrong

it is an

80

it is best	it is impossible
it is better	it is interesting
it is better than	it is likely
it is better to	it is more likely
it is certain	it is more than likely
it is certainly	it is most likely
it is certainly not	it is my intention
it is clear	it is my opinion
it is easier	it is my pleasure
it is easier than	it is necessary
it is easier to	it is nice
it is easy	it is no good
it is fair	it is not a question of
it is fair to say	it is not bad
it is good	it is not certain
it is hard	it is not clear
it is harder	it is not easy
it is harder than	it is not fair
it is harder to	it is not fair to say
it is imperative	it is not good
it is important	it is not important

it is not impossible

it is not impossible ....

it is not likely ....

it is not my intention ....

it is not my opinion ....

it is not necessary ....

it is not nice ....

it is not only ....

it is not possible ....

it is not quite right ....

it is not quite right to say ....

it is not quite true ....

it is not quite true to say ....

it is not right ....

it is not so ....

it is not true ....

it is not true to say ....

it is not wise ....

it is not worthwhile ....

it is not wrong ....

it is only ....

it is possible ....

it is probable ....

it is probably ....

it is probably true to say ....

it is quite likely ....

it is quite possible ....

it is quite probable ....

it is quite right ....

it is quite true ....

it is quite wrong ....

it is right ....

it is terrible ....

it is time ....

it is tragic ....

it is true ....

it is true to say ....

it is unnecessary ....

it is worse ....

it is worse than ....

82

it is worthwhile ....

it is wrong ....

it may be possible ....

it might be possible ....

it must be possible ....

it seems that the ....

it seems to me ....

it should be possible ....

it was ....

Note: most of the groupings which start *it is* can be adapted by substituting *was* for *is*.

it were ....

it will be possible ....

it would be possible ....

item on the agenda ....

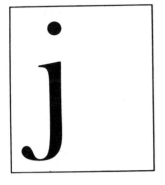

j

jack of all trades .....

jet set .....

joint-stock banks .....

joint-stock company .....

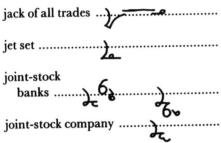

joys of spring .....

judge and jury .....

jury service .....

just a minute .....

just about .....

just in time .....

just so .....

just the same .....

juvenile court .....

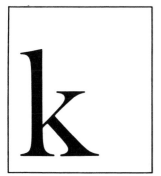

keep left ....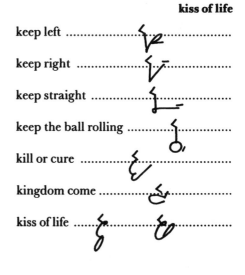

keep right ....

keep straight ....

keep the ball rolling ....

kill or cure ....

keep down ....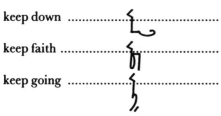

keep faith ....

keep going ....

kingdom come ....

kiss of life ....

labour costs

labour of love

labour relations

ladies and gentlemen

lap of luxury

large amount

large measure

large number

larger and larger

laser beams

last autumn

last bus

last but not least

last but by no means least

last fight

last fling

last Friday

last gasp

last hope

last lap

last laugh

last minute

last Monday

last month

last night

last payment

last piece

last post

last request

last resort

last rites

last Saturday

last second

last spring

last straw

last Sunday

last thing	leaders of industry
last Thursday	leading light
last time	leading question
last train	league table
last Tuesday	led astray
last way	left, right and centre
last Wednesday	left to right
last week	left wing
last will and testament	legal action
last winter	legal advice
last wish	legal requirements
last word	legal tender
last year	leisure time
later on	length and breadth
later than	less and less
latest craze	let me
latest fashion	let me know
latest figures	let me say
laughing-stock	let me see
law and order	let slip
Leader of the Opposition	

let the side down ......

let us ......

let us know ......

letter of authority ......

letter of enquiry ......

letter of the law ......

letters of administration ......

level best ......

level crossing ......

level of investment ......

life and limb ......

life insurance ......

life sentence ......

light sentence ......

light work ......

limited company ......

limited liability ......

line of enquiry ......

line of least resistance ......

line scanner ......

lines of communication ......

lion's share ......

lip-service ......

liquid assets ......

little by little ......

little point ......

live wire ......

livestock insurance ......

Lloyd's of London ......

local authority ......

local council ......

local councillor ......

local productivity agreement ......

local productivity deal ......

local trader ......

lock, stock and barrel ......

long ago ......

long before ......

long distance ......

long life ......

long period ......

long speech	lower and lower ....
long story	lower than ....
long suffering	lowest cost ....
long term	lowest terms ....
long time	
long time ago	
long time since	
long way	
longer and longer	
loss of trade	
lost cause	
lost orders	
lot of money	
low cost	
low down	
low ebb	
low pressure	
low productivity	
low profile	
low proportion	
low tide	

Madam Chairman ....

made a statement ....

made the point ....

made to measure ....

majority decision ....

majority verdict ....

make a statement ....

make amends ....

make merry ....

make or break ....

make sure ....

make the most of ....

make way ....

making merry ....

making sure ....

man and woman ....

man in the middle ....

man in the street ....

man of the moment ....

man of the people ....

man of the world ....

man on the spot ....

man or woman ....

man to man ....

man, woman and child ....

management committee ....

managing
    director ....

manner of speaking ....

manufacturing company ....

manufacturing industry ....

manufacturing investment ....

many more ....

many people ....

many things ....

margin of profit ....

marine
    insurance ....

mark my words ....

mark time ....

market-place ....

market research ....

matter for concern ....

matter of concern ....

matter of contract ....

matter of fact ....

matter of interest ....

matter of trust ....

maximum efficiency ....

medical evidence ....

Member of Parliament ....

member of the association ....

member of the committee ....

member of the council ....

member of the general public ....

member of the jury ....

members of the jury ....

member of the public ....

members of the public ....

men and women ....

men or women ....

men, women and children ....

metropolitan borough ....

metropolitan council ....

middle-aged ....

middle man ....

midsummer madness ....

miles an hour ....

miles per hour ....

mind over matter ....

mining industry ....

Minister of State ....

Mr and Mrs ....

Mr Chairman ....

mixed bag ....

mixed blessing ....

mixed fortunes ....

mob rule

mob rule

moment of truth

Monday afternoon

Monday evening

Monday morning

Monday next

Monday night

monetary control

monetary policy

money supply

monkey business

month after month

month to month

monthly account

monthly payment

monthly statement

moral responsibility

more and more

more important

more or less

more people

more than

more than necessary

more things

more's the pity

mortal remains

most important

most of all

most of them

most of us

most of you

most people

most things

mother-in-law

motor accident

motor bike

motor car

motor-car accident

motor-car industry

motor-car insurance

motor cycle

motor industry ....

motor racing ....

motor show ....

motor sport ....

motor-vehicle
insurance ....

move with the times ....

much importance ....

much less ....

much less than ....

much more ....

much more than ....

multilateral disarmament ....

multilateral discussions ....

multilateral talks ....

multi-million dollar ....

multi-million pound ....

multi-storey building ....

multi-storey car park ....

multi-system ....

music centre ....

music lover ....

musical evening ....

musical instrument ....

my account ....

my attention ....

my authority ....

my intention ....

my word ....

n

name and address ......

names and addresses ......

national anthem ......

national defence ......

national emergency ......

national executive ......

National Health Service ......

National Insurance ......

national interest ......

national problem ......

national savings ......

National Savings
   Certificates ......

national security ......

national service ......

natural causes ......

94

nature cure ......

nature reserve ......

near and far ......

near future ......

near miss ......

near the ......

near the mark ......

near thing ......

nearer and nearer ......

nearer than ......

nearer the ......

nearest and dearest ......

nearest point ......

neck and crop ......

neck and neck ......

needless to say ......

negative film ......

negative reaction ......

negative result ......

net loss ......

net profit ......

never again	next thing
never before	next Thursday
never once	next time
never say die	next to nothing
never since	next Tuesday
next autumn	next Wednesday
next day	next week
next door	next winter
next evening	next year
next Friday	night after night
next meeting	night-work
next Monday	nitty-gritty
next month	no authority
next morning	no chance
next of kin	no charge
next Saturday	no-claims bonus
next spring	no defence
next step	no delay
next summer	no doubt
next Sunday	no fewer than
next term	no laughing matter

no less

no less ....

no less than ....

no longer ....

no more ....

no more than ....

no point ....

no sooner said than done ..

no such thing ....

no time ....

no trouble ....

no way ....

no-go area ....

no one else ....

normal service ...

normal terms ....

normal trading ....

north coast ....

north of the border ......

not all ....

not at all ....

not clear ....

not enough ....

not long ....

not much ....

not much more ....

not much more than ....

not only ....

not right ....

not so ....

not sorry ....

not sure ....

not valid ....

not wrong ....

not yet ....

nothing else ....

nothing less than ....

nothing more than ......

nothing of the kind ....

nothing of the sort ....

nothing on earth ....

now and again ....

now and then ....

nowhere else ....

nuclear arms ....

nuclear arms race ....

nuclear bomb ....

nuclear deterrent ....

nuclear disarmament ....

nuclear energy ....

nuclear expansion ....

nuclear explosion ....

nuclear fission ....

nuclear fuel ....

nuclear fusion ....

nuclear holocaust ....

nuclear physicist ....

nuclear physics ....

nuclear power ....

nuclear propulsion ....

nuclear reaction ....

nuclear reactor ....

nuclear shelter ....

nuclear test ....

nuclear-test ban ....

nuclear-test ban treaty ....

nuclear war ....

nuclear weapons ....

nuclear winter ....

null and void ....

number of ....

number of accidents ....

number of days ....

number of people ....

number of points ....

number of questions ....

number of things ....

number of times ....

number of ways ....

number of weeks ....

number of words ....

number of years ....

nuts and bolts ....

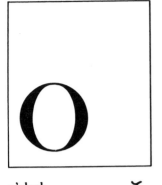

o'clock ....

odd man out ....

odds against ....

odds and ends ....

odds-on ....

of a ....

of an ....

of course ....

of that ....

of the ....

of them ....

of these ....

of this ....

of those ....

of us ....

of you ....

off and on ....

off course ....

off the ......

off the air ....

off the cuff ....

off the end ....

off the mark ....

off the record ....

off the scent ....

office computer ....

office staff ......

office worker ....

old boy ......

old flame ....

old friend ....

old girl ....

old hand ....

old lady ....

old man ......

old people ....

old school ....

98

old school tie ....

old soldier ....

old story ....

old wives' tale ....

old woman ....

on a shoestring ....

on and off ....

on bail ....

on balance ....

on behalf of ....

on call ....

on condition ....

on demand ....

on duty ....

on fire ....

on good authority ....

on loan ....

on occasions ....

on one hand ....

on reflection ....

on remand ....

on sufferance ....

on target ....

on tenterhooks ....

on the ....

on the air ....

on the ball ....

on the boil ....

on the breadline ....

on the break ....

on the brink ....

on the cards ....

on the carpet ....

on the contrary ....

on the day ....

on the dole ....

on the dot ....

on the dotted line ....

on the double ....

on the face of it ....

on the fence ....

on the floor ....

on the go

on the go

on the inside

on the job

on the left

on the level

on the line

on the map

on the mat

on the move

on the nail

on the off-chance

on the offensive

on the one hand

on the one side

on the other hand

on the other side

on the outside

on the question of

on the quiet

on the rack

on the receiving end

on the reverse

on the right

on the right foot

on the right hand

on the right side

on the right tack

on the right track

on the road

on the rocks

on the roof

on the run

on the safe side

on the same side

on the side

on the sidelines

on the spot

on the spur of the
moment

on the table

on the trail

on the understanding

100

on the up and up	once upon a time
on the wagon	one and the same
on the warpath	one and the same thing
on the way	one by one
on the wing	one thing
on the wrong foot	one thing after another
on the wrong side	open air
on the wrong tack	open-and-shut case
on the wrong track	open arms
on trial	open-ended
once a day	open up
once a month	operating costs
once a week	optical illusion
once a year	or a
once again	or an
once and for all	or anything
once before	or else
once in a lifetime	or less
once in a while	or more
once more	or not
once or twice	or nothing

101

or so	ought to have been
or something	out for the count
or that	out of
or the	out of action
or these	out of bounds
or this	out of breath
or those	out of business
order form	out of commission
ordered to make restitution	out of court
ordinary dividend	out of date
ordinary shares	out of hand
other end	out of joint
other offences	out of mind
other people	out of order
other things	out of place
other things being equal	out of pocket
other things equal	out of season
other ways	out of sight
our company	out of sorts
our order	out of step
	out of stock

out of that

over that

out of the

over the

out of the ordinary

over the border

out of the picture

over the hill

out of the question

over the last month

out of the way

over the last week

out of these

over the last year

out of this

over the moon

out of this world

over the past month

out of those

over the past week

out of time

over the past year

out of turn

over the rainbow

out of work

over the worst

outstanding amount

over their/there

oven-ready

over their heads

over a period of time

over these

over and above

over this

over and done with

over those

over and over

overdraft facilities

over and over again

overseas company

over it

overseas market

103

overseas sales

overseas sales ....⏑⏑⏑................

overseas trade ....⏑⏑⏑................

overwhelming evidence ....⏑⏑⏑..........

overwhelming majority ......⏑⏑⏑..........

overwhelming odds .....⏑⏑⏑...............

overwhelming support ....⏑⏑⏑...........

owing to the fact that .⏑⏑⏑.........⏑⏑⏑....

p

panic measures

panic stations

par excellence

parish council

parking-meter

parking space

parliamentary privilege

parrot-fashion

part and parcel

part-exchange

part of

part payment

part time

part-time course

part-time education

part-time employment

part-time job

participating preference
  shares

parting shot

parts of the world

party line

party piece

party policy

pass by

pass on

pass through

passed away

passed by

passed unanimously

passing by

passing car

passing moment

passing motorist

passing phase

passing through

past and present

past decade

past decade ....

past month ....

past week ....

past year ....

pattern of crime ....

pave/paving the way ....

pay-as-you-earn ....

pay bargaining ....

pay-claim ....

pay increase ....

pay negotiations ....

pay restraint ....

pay settlement ....

payment in kind ....

payment in lieu ....

peace and quiet ....

peace-offering ....

peace talks ....

peaceful solution ....

peculiar circumstances ....

pedestrian crossing ....

pedestrian precinct ....

per annum ....

per cent ....

perfect example ....

perfect harmony ....

perfect solution ....

perfect stranger ....

personal accident and
   illness insurance ....

personal assistant ....

personal computer ....

personnel officer ....

photo finish ....

pins and needles ....

plain sailing ....

plant and machinery ....

play ball ....

played out ....

players' entrance ....

plead guilty ....

plead not guilty ....

106

pleaded guilty	political party	
pleaded not guilty	political party conference	
please quote	poor relation	
pleased to say	poor show	
pleased to see	pop music	
pleased to see you	pop record	
plenty of time	positive reaction	
poetic justice	positive result	
poetic licence	post-code	
point of departure	post-mortem examination	
point of law	post office	
point of no return	postal order	
point of order	*poste restante*	
point of view	pot luck	
point out	pounds a month	
pointed out	pounds a week	
points of view	pounds a year	
poles apart	power of attorney	
police court	preference shares	
police officer	preferential treatment	
police station	preliminary enquiry	

107

premature baby

premature retirement

prepaid envelope

prepaid order card

prepaid order form

present company excepted

present day

present time

press on

previous conviction

previous day

previous decade

previous month

previous week

previous year

price decrease

price increase

price reduction

prices and incomes policy

pride of place

prime example

Prime Minister

prime suspect

prior arrangement

prior commitment

prior knowledge

prior need

prior occasion

private army

private correspondence

private matter

private property

private room

private sector

private soldier

private talk

productivity bonus

productivity deal

profit and loss account

profit margin

profit sharing

108

promised land

promissory note

prompt attention

proper perspective

proposal form

pros and cons

public concern

public convenience

public debate

public expenditure

public house

public inquiry

public interest

public money

public order

public pressure

public property

public sector

public servant

public service

public-service vehicle

public speaker

public speaking

public spending

public-spending cuts

public transport

pure and simple

purse strings

put on

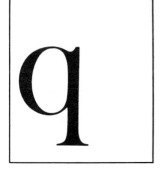

question time ....

quick march ....

quick off the mark ....

quick on the uptake ....

quick profit ....

quick settlement ....

quick thinking ....

quick turnover ....

quicker and quicker ....

quicker than ....

quick's the word ....

quite a long time ....

quite a long way ....

quite a long while ....

quite a lot ....

quite a lot of ....

quite a short time ....

quite a short way ....

quite a short while ....

quite all right ....

quite aware ....

quite bad ....

quite big ....

quite capable ....

quite certain ....

quite clear ....

quite correct ....

quite full ....

quite good ....

quite important ....

quite impossible ....

quite large ....

quite likely ....

quite nasty ....

quite near ....

quite nice ....

quite old ....

110

quite possible ....

quite quick ....

quite quickly ....

quite ridiculous ....

quite right ....

quite slow ....

quite slowly ....

quite small ....

quite so ....

quite soon ....

quite sorry ....

quite sorry to say ....

quite sorry to see ....

quite sure ....

quite terrible ....

quite true ....

quite wrong ....

quite young ....

race relations ....

racial disadvantage ....

racial discrimination ....

racial equality ....

racial harmony ....

racial minority ....

racial prejudice ....

racial strife ....

racial tension ....

racial violence ....

rack and ruin ....

raffle ticket ....

rail station ....

railway station ....

rank and file ....

rank outsider ....

rapid growth ....

rapid results ....

rapid strides ....

rarefied atmosphere ....

rat race ....

rate capping ....

rate demand ....

rate of exchange ....

rate of interest ....

rate rebate ....

rateable value ....

rather less ....

rather less than ....

rather more ....

rather more than ....

rather nice ....

rather pleasant ....

rather than ....

rating and valuation ....

raving mad ....

raw materials ....

read and adopted ....

read/reading between the lines ....

rear seat ....

reasonable doubt ....

recent accident ....

recent bereavement ....

recent case ....

recent change ....

recent death ....

recent letter ....

recent order ....

recorded delivery ....

recruiting drive ....

red alert ....

red flag ....

red herring ....

Red Indian ....

red-letter day ....

red light ....

redeemable preference shares ....

reduced profits ....

reduced sentence ....

redundancy pay ....

refer back ....

referred back ....

referring to ....

registered post ....

registrar of companies ....

regret to inform you ....

regular customer ....

regular savings ....

reign of terror ....

relatively speaking ....

remanded in custody ....

remanded on bail ....

reply-paid ....

report and accounts ....

residents' association ....

restrictive practices ....

retail shop ....

113

retail trade	rock and roll
retrograde step	rock bottom
retrospective legislation	rock-bottom price
return to sender	rolling stone
rhyme or reason	room number
rich man	room service
right of way	rooted to the ground
right or wrong	rooted to the spot
right place	rough-and-ready
right way	rough-and-tumble
right wing	rough diamond
ring of truth	rough ground
rising costs	royal borough
rising damp	royal charter
rising ground	royal command
rising prices	royal commission
risk capital	royal family
river bank	royal palace
river bed	royal prerogative
river crossing	rub shoulders
road-traffic offence	rubber ball

running track

rubber stamp ....⟋ᗱ⟍........|...........

run of the mill ....⟋ᗰᒼ................

run riot ....⟋ᐱ......................

running battle ....⟋ᗷᒑ...............

running costs ......⟋ᗱ⟋......................

running shoes ....⟋ᗱ⟋...................

running track ....⟋ᓇᒼ...................

115

safe and sound

safety first

same again

satisfactory results

Saturday afternoon

Saturday evening

Saturday morning

Saturday next

Saturday night

savings bank

school-leaver

school-leaving age

seat-belt

second-best

second bond

second chance

second fiddle

second-hand

second nature

secondary picketing

secondary school

secondary strike

secretarial training

Secretary of State

seems to have been

seen better days

selective strike action

self-financing productivity
  deal

send us

send you

sending you

separate rooms

serious accident

serious matter

set aside

set the ball rolling

set the scene

set the stage

set the wheels in motion

set up

several enquiries

several occasions

several people

several things

several times

several years

several years ago

severe sentence

sex assault

sex offence

sex offender

sex pervert

sexual intercourse

share account

share and share alike

share out

sheet-anchor

shift work

shift worker

ship-building industry

ship canal

shipping agent

shipping industry

shipping lane

shipping line

shipping office

ship's officer

shopkeeper's insurance

shopping area

short and sweet

short change

short cut

short list

short measure

short sentence

short shrift

short-staffed

short supply

117

short term

short term ....

short time ....

short walk ....

short way ....

short work ....

shorter and shorter ....

shot in the arm ....

shot in the dark ....

shoulder to shoulder .....

show business ....

show of hands ....

sick and tired ....

sick-leave ....

sick to death ....

side by side ....

sight for sore eyes ....

sign of the times ....

sign on the dotted line ....

silicon chip ....

simple matter ....

sincere apologies ...

sink or swim ......

sister-in-law ....

sisters-in-law ....

sitting duck ....

sitting pretty ....

sitting target ....

sleeping partner ....

slow down ....

slow going ....

slow motion ....

slow off the mark ....

slow on the draw ....

slow on the uptake ......

slow up ....

slower and slower ...

small print ....

small talk ....

smaller and smaller ...

smaller than ...

snap up ....

so far ....

118

so far as ....

so far as I am concerned ....

so far, so good ....

so many ....

so much ....

so that ....

so to say ....

so to speak ....

social committee ....

social problem ....

social security ....

social service ....

social system ....

social worker ....

soft option ....

solitary confinement ....

somehow or other ....

some measure ....

some more ....

some other ....

some people ....

some things ....

some time or other ....

something else ....

something more than ....

sooner or later ....

sooner than ....

sound as a bell ....

sour grapes ....

south coast ....

south of the border ....

spadework ....

spanner into the works ....

spirit of the law ....

spoken word ....

square peg ....

staff of life ....

staggering loss ....

stamping-ground ....

stand by ....

stand down ....

stand fast ....

stand up

stand up ....

standard of living ....

standard procedure ....

standing order ....

stands to reason ....

start the ball rolling ....

start up ....

state of affairs ....

state of play ....

state of the economy ....

state of things ....

state secret ....

statement of accounts ....

steady as a rock ....

steer clear ....

step by step ....

stick in the mud ....

sticky wicket ....

sting in the tail ....

Stock Exchange ....

stock-in-trade ....

stocks and shares ....

stone-deaf ....

stone's throw ....

stop short ....

storm in a teacup ....

straight and narrow ....

straight as a die ....

straight as an arrow ....

straight away ....

straight line ....

strange thing ....

streak of lightning ....

streets ahead ....

stresses and strains ....

strictly speaking ....

strike action ....

stumbling-block ....

subject to contract ....

subsidiary company ....

120

such things ....

sum of money ....

sums of money ....

Sunday afternoon ....

Sunday evening ....

Sunday morning ....

Sunday next ....

Sunday night ....

surplus profits ....

suspended sentence ....

suspicious character ....

suspicious circumstances ....

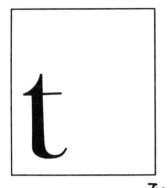

take advantage of ....

take away ....

take care ....

take care of ....

take cover ....

take down ....

take exception ....

take in ....

take into consideration ....

take into custody ....

take issue ....

take issue with ....

take kindly ....

take leave ....

take off ....

take offence ....

take on ....

take out ....

take over ....

take-over bid ....

take pains ....

take part ....

take sides ....

take stock ....

take the liberty ....

take the opportunity ....

take the point ....

take the rough with the smooth ....

take this opportunity ....

take time ....

take turns ....

take up ....

taken as read ....

taken into consideration ....

taken into custody ....

tall story ....

tax-free	test case
technical ability	test-tube
technical adviser	test-tube baby
technical college	thank you
technical difficulties	thank you for your enquiry
technical drawing	thank you for your letter
technical terms	thank you for your order
technical training	thank you for your recent enquiry
technological age	thank you for your recent order
technological change	
technological revolution	thank you very much
technological skills	thankless task
teething troubles	thanks to
telephone bill	that is right
telephone call	that is to say
telephone conversation	that is wrong
telephone exchange	that that
telex network	that the
tell the truth	that their/there
temporary measure	that these
terms of reference	that this

that those ....

the chairman said ....

the end ....

the ends of the earth ....

the face of the earth ....

the fact of the matter ....

the fact that ....

the facts of the matter ....

the following extract ....

the following is an extract ....

the last straw ....

the more the merrier ....

the other day ....

the other side ....

the other side of the coin ....

the other side of the story ....

the other side of the world ....

the salt of the earth ....

the same old story ....

the sands of time ....

the sooner the better ....

the year dot ....

then and now ....

there and back ....

there is a ....

there is a possibility ....

there is an ....

there is another point ....

there is another possibility ....

there is another thing ....

there is no doubt ....

there is no point ....

there is no possibility ....

there is no reason ....

there is the possibility ....

there was a ....

there was an ....

there was another point ....

there was another possibility ....

there was another thing ....

there was no doubt

there was no point

there was no possibility

these days

these things

they will

they would

third-party fire and theft insurance

Third World

this afternoon

this and that

this company

this evening

this matter

this month

this morning

this or that

this order

this summer

this, that and the other

this time

this way

this week

this winter

this year

those days

those things

through the

throughout the year

thumbs down

thumbs up

Thursday afternoon

Thursday evening

Thursday morning

Thursday next

Thursday night

tickled pink

tight control

tight corner

tight fit

tight spot

tight spot ....

tight squeeze ....

time after time ....

time and again ....

time and tide ....

time and time again ....

time flies ....

time immemorial ....

time-lag ....

time to spare ....

times a day ....

times to come ....

tit for tat ....

to a great extent ....

to a greater extent ....

to a large extent ....

to an extent ....

to and fro ....

to balance ....

to be ....

to be asked ....

to be careful ....

to be done ....

to be exact ....

to be right ....

to be sorry ....

to be sure ....

to be taken ....

to be taken into
    consideration ....

to be told ....

to be wrong ....

to become ....

to begin ....

to believe ....

to bring ....

to build ....

to build up ....

to carry ....

to change ....

to charge ....

to check ....

126

to come	to say the least
to conclude	to see
to cover	to sell
to cut a long story short	to send
to drive	to serve
to get	to show
to give	to sign
to go	to some extent
to govern	to spare
to grow	to speak
to hand	to spend
to learn	to stand
to make	to start
to mark	to state
to mean	to stay
to meet	to steal
to my mind	to stop
to my way of thinking	to suggest
to need	to that
to save	to the
to say	to the fore

127

to them

to these

to think

to this

to those

to walk

to wish

to work

tomorrow afternoon

tomorrow morning

tomorrow night

too much

tooth and nail

top brass

top dog

top drawer

top level

top price

top priority

top quality

top rung

touch and go

touch up

touch wood

tourist industry

tower block

tower of strength

town and country

town centre

town council

town councillor

town hall

track record

track suit

trade and industry

trade directory

trade unions

trading loss

trading profit

traffic offence

train crash

train driver ....

transport system ....

travel expenses ....

travellers' cheques ....

travelling time ....

treasure

  trove ....

trend-setter ....

trend-setting ....

trial and error ....

trials and tribulations ....

true-blue ....

true to form ....

true to say ....

true to type ....

Tuesday afternoon ....

Tuesday evening ....

Tuesday morning ....

Tuesday next ....

Tuesday night ....

turn and turn about ....

turn down ....

turn over ....

turn round ....

turn tail ....

twice as much ....

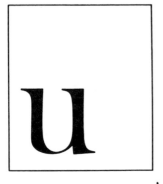

unable to obtain ....

unanimous decision ....

unanimous verdict ....

unconditional acceptance ....

unconditional discharge ....

unconditional surrender ....

unconfirmed report ....

under equipped ....

under fire ....

under insured ....

under lock and key ....

under pressure ....

under staffed ....

under the ....

under the counter ....

under the influence ....

under separate cover ....

under way ....

underground train ....

unilateral action ....

unilateral
   disarmament ....

United Kingdom ....

up against it ....

up and coming ....

up and down ....

up and up ....

updated ....

up in arms ....

up market ....

up to date ....

up to scratch ....

up to the mark ....

up to the minute ....

upon reflection ....

upper case ....

upper class ....

upper hand ....

upper reaches ....

ups and downs ....

upside down ....

urgent business ....

urgent consideration ....

urgent matter ....

urgently required ....

used again ....

used by ....

used for ....

used less ....

used more ....

used most ....

used to be ....

used up ....

utter chaos ....

utter rubbish ....

utterly ridiculous ....

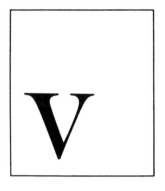

valuable asset ....

value-added tax ....

VAT ....

value for money ....

vanishing-point ....

vanishing trick ....

vantage point ....

vast area ....

vast expanse ....

vast expense ....

vast experience ....

venture capital ....

venture to suggest ....

verdict of accidental
death ....

very bad ....

very big ....

very careful ....

very careless ....

very costly ....

very different ....

very difficult ....

very good ....

very great ....

very kind ....

very large ....

very long ....

very near ....

very nice ....

very poor ....

very positive ....

very similar ....

very small ....

very soon ....

very sorry ....

very strange ...

very strong ....

very sure ....

very true ....

very truly yours ....

very vague ....

very vivid ....

very wasteful ....

very weak ....

very welcome ....

very well ....

vested interest ....

victim of circumstance ....

video cassette ....

video disc ....

video display unit ....

video film ....

video recorder ....

video screen ....

video tape ....

viewdata ....

vis-à-vis ....

visible earnings ....

vital statistics ....

volume of trade ....

voluntary contribution ....

voluntary donation ....

voluntary society ....

vote of thanks ....

wage demand ....

wage earner ....

wage freeze ....

wage packet ....

wage restraint ....

wait a minute ....

wait and see ....

wake up ....

walks of life ....

wall to wall ....

washed up ....

waste ground ....

waste of time ....

waste paper ....

waste product ....

wasted effort ....

water pressure ....

way of life ....

ways and means ....

we are afraid ....

we are certain ....

we are glad ....

we are going ....

we are pleased ....

we are pleased to know ....

we are pleased to say ....

we are pleased to see ....

we are sending you ....

we are sorry ....

we are sorry to say ....

we are sorry to see ....

we are sure ....

we are thinking ....

we believe ....

we can ....

we can say ....

we can see ....

we consider ....

we enclose ....

we expect ....

we have much pleasure ....

we have pleasure ....

we must say ....

we must see ....

we prefer ....

we presume ....

we propose ....

we regret to say ....

we regret to state ....

we saw ....

we say ....

we see ....

we should be pleased ....

we suppose ....

we thank you ....

we were quite right ....

we were quite wrong ....

we were sorry ....

we were sure ....

we were very sorry ....

we wish to say ....

we wish to see ....

we wish to state ....

wear and tear ....

wedding-day ....

wedding-ring ....

Wednesday
   afternoon ....

Wednesday evening ....

Wednesday last ....

Wednesday morning ....

Wednesday next ....

Wednesday night ....

weed-killer ....

weeks ago ....

well and truly ....

well aware ....

well done ....

well known ....

135

west coast ....

what is ....

what is best ....

what is better ....

what is more ....

what is more to the point ....

what is the ....

what is the matter ....

what is the point ....

what is worse ....

wheels within wheels ....

when all is said and done ....

where is ....

where is the ....

where the ....

where was ....

where was the ....

where
we were ....

where
were we ....

where
were you ....

where
you were ....

whether or not ....

which can ....

which could ....

which is ....

which should ....

which was ....

which were ....

which will ....

which would ....

white as a sheet ....

wholesale market ....

wholesale trade ....

wide of the mark ....

wide range ....

wide ranging ....

wide world ....

will you require ....

window-dressing ....

wise after the event ....

with all due respect ....

with effect from ....

with hindsight ....

with me ....

with the ....

with reference to ....

with reference to your
   enquiry ....

with reference to your
   letter ....

with reference to your
   order ....

with regard to ....

with regret ....

with us ....

with you ....

within reach ....

within reason ....

within striking distance ....

without doubt ....

without effort ....

without exception ....

without question ....

witness for the defence ....

witness for the
   prosecution ....

wits' end ....

word of mouth ....

word processing ....

word-processing ability ....

word processor ....

words a minute ....

words per minute ....

work to rule ....

working class ....

working relationship ....

worked up ....

world bank ....

world markets ....

world
   trade ....

worlds apart ....

worm's-eye view ....

worse and worse ....

worse for wear ....

worse luck

worse luck ....⟋..................   worth considering ....⌐⌐....⟋..........

worth consideration ....⌐⌐...........   written agreement ......⟋⟍⟍.................

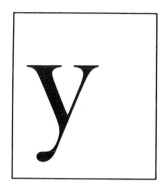

year after year

years and years

year ended

year to year

years ago

years of age

years old

yesterday afternoon

yesterday evening

yesterday morning

yet again

yet more

you expect

you say

young couple

young lady

young man

young men

young people

young person

young woman

young women

your account

your attention

your early attention

your earliest convenience

your enquiry

your order

your reply

your request

your requirements

yours faithfully

yours sincerely

yours truly

yours very truly